Excellence in English

Preparation for Selection Tests

Year 2

Peter Howard

Peter Howard is an Australian ex-primary school principal and author of many text books and teaching aids. A number of his works are published in the UK, USA, Canada and Asian countries.

Excellence in English Year 2
© Peter Howard 2011
Published by Coroneos Publications 2011

ISBN   978-1-86294-236-3

This book is available from recognised booksellers or contact:

Coroneos Publications

Telephone: (02) 9838 9265   **Facsimile:** (02) 9838 8982
Business Address: 2/195 Prospect Highway Seven Hills 2147
Website: www.coroneos.com.au
E-mail: info@fivesenseseducation.com.au

Foreword

Excellence in English Year 2 is the second of a series aimed at primary children to help improve their English. There are many challenging exercises that will extend their vocabulary, grammar, reading and thinking skills. The systematic practice will give confidence to those who may later sit for entrance or scholarship examinations which test English and General Aptitude.

It is suggested that a child works through the book sequentially rather than jumping from one section to another. A dictionary should be consulted to avoid guesswork- especially when the meaning of a multiple- choice word is not known.

Answers are provided in the centre section for ease of removal. When using this book at home or school, it may be a temptation for a child to look at answers if they remain in the book.

Peter Howard

Contents

Reading (Revision of letter sounds)

Vocabulary

Reading (Revision of Letter Sounds)

Using One Vowel

Use one vowel (a, e, I, o, or u) and then one more letter to complete each word.

1   w .... a spider's home

2   p .... a farm animal

3   c .... baby's bed

4   b .... used for cricket

5   p .... a plant grows in it.

6   m .... used for cleaning

7   f .... animal

8   s .... It is in the sky.

9   v .... small truck

10 h .... farm bird

11 p .... used to write

12 l .... top of a box

13 b .... used for sleeping

14 r .... small animal

15 l .... wood from a tree

16 f .... A shark has one.

17 f .... not thin

18 t .... upper part

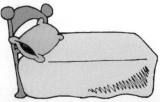
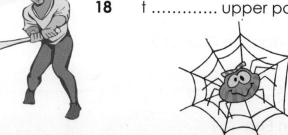

Use one vowel and another letter to make each word. Be careful, as the vowel may or may not come first.

19 f ....g   It flies from a pole.

20 g .... f   game using clubs

21 n ....t   bird's home

22 p .... m   a fruit

23 b ....t   worn round waist

24 s .... n   It covers the body.

25 p .... m   Baby rides in it.

26 s ....ps We climb them.

27 s .... m   move in water

28 p ....d   small area of water

29 s .... nk animal

Use one vowel (a, e, I, o, or u) and then one more letter to complete each word.

1   The basket was made of c......ne.

2   Toothpaste or face cream can come in a t.......be.

3   The number before ten is n......ne.

4   The flag is flying from a p......le.

5   Some dogs will b........te you if you are not careful.

6   The d.........te was the tenth of June.

7   A m.........le is half a horse and half a donkey.

8   The bl.........de of a knife is often sharp.

Now try two words in the same sentence.

9   Small c.........bes with spots on them are called d......ce.

10 The gr......pe is a fruit that grows on a v........ne.

11 The dog buried his b......ne under the r......se bushes.

12 Shaun has f.....ve white mice in a c......ge.

13 On the pl.......te was a whole chocolate c........ke.

14 Can you play a t......ne on your fl......te?

15 I have to fix the br.........kes on my b........ke.

16 For a j.......ke I put on a false n.......se to frighten my brother.

 © Peter Howard 2011   Published by Coroneos Publications

Using Two Vowels

Use two vowels together in each word after reading the clue.

ee	1	part of your foot	h	2	a kind of meat	b........
	3	Apples grow on it.	t.........	4	found on a bed	sh......
ea	5	a drink	t.........	6	a bird's mouth	b........
	7	part of milk	c..............	8	a large meal	f........
oa	9	animal with horns	g.........	10	used for washing	s........
	11	baby horse	f.............	12	part of your neck	t.........
ou	13	to yell	s..............	14	It floats in the sky	c.......
	15	We sit on it.	c...........	16	bread is made from it.	f.........
ai	17	It runs on rails.	t............	18	a slow creature	s............
	19	It makes us wet.	r...........	20	used to catch fish	b.........
oi	21	metal money	c...........	22	heat up water	b...........
	23	Snakes do this.	c............	24	end of a pencil	p...........
oo	25	used to make jumpers	w......	26	We read it.	b..............
	27	worn over the head	h..........	28	A hammer is one.	t.........
au	29	a boy's name	P...........	30	a small ship	l.............
	31	pull	h............	32	We put it on food.	s.........

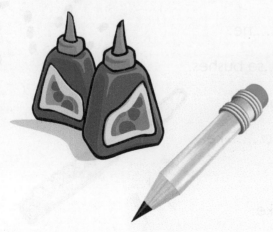

Using One Vowel and Another Letter

Use the two letters together in each word after reading the clue.

ar	1	a fierce sea creature s......		2	The sun is one. s.........
	3	not blunt s.........		4	worn round the neck s......
er	5	He cuts hair b.........		6	used in cooking h.......
	7	It flows to the sea r..........		8	a type of plant f........
ir	9	a young woman g.........		10	the number after 29 t.....
	11	worn by a woman s.........		12	not clean d.........
ow	13	a black bird c..........		14	It can fall in winter. s.......
	15	You sleep on it. p..........		16	a colour y............
aw	17	a baby deer f...........		18	part of a car's paw c........
	19	It is an area of grass l........		20	a hunting bird h.........
ow	21	a bird that flies at night o.......		22	Dogs do it. g..........
	23	worn by a king or queen c........		24	We dry with it. t...........
or	25	It fits in a bottle. c..........		26	a bird with long legs s......
	27	opposite to south n..........		28	We eat with one. f.........
ay	29	used to carry drinks t...........		30	opposite to leave s........
	31	We do this on a piano p......		32	grass cut for feed h.........

Begin Words by Blending Two Letters Together

Begin each word with a blend of two letters.

Cross out each pair of letters as you use them.

st	fl	sp	dr	fr	gl	cr	pl

1   We drink water from a ....ass.

2   My sister wore a new ....ess to the party.

3   A ....ider spins a web to catch insects.

4   A ....ump is all that is left on an old tree.

5   To keep water in a basin we use a ....ug.

6   Look both ways before you ....oss the road.

7   Dad ....owns when he is not happy.

8   To dive under the sea you put on some ....ippers.

br	cl	st	sp	dr	gl

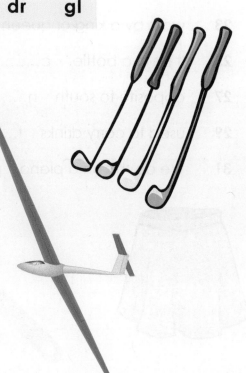

9   Mum ....ives us to school in the car.

10 A ....anner is used to undo nuts.

11 My brother has a set of golf ....ubs.

12 A ....ider is a plane with no motor.

13 A ....ag is a male deer.

14 I ....ush my teeth after meals.

End Words by Blending Two Letters Together

End each word with a blend of two letters.

Cross out each pair of letters as you use them.

ng ch sh ck nk sk nt st

1   A du............ is a bird that swims.

2   You can keep pet fish in a ta............ .

3   An actor may wear a ma............ on his face.

4   The king put his gold in a che.............. .

5   I heard the balloon burst with a ba............ .

6   The te.............. kept us dry for the night in the rain.

7   My dog eats from a di................ .

8   A bit............is a female dog.

st nt ng ng nk nk ck ck sh sh ch ch

9   A so............. is made to go on ea............ foot.

10 Fre............. green tea grows on a low bu.............. .

11 My dog will dri............ water and pa.......... when he is hot.

12 Did you wat.......... Australia come fir............ in the rowing race?

13 When you wi............ one eye it is like blinki............. .

14 My Aunt wears a large, bla.......... opal ri.......... on her finger.

Make New Words

Add one letter to make each new word. Use only the letters given to you on the left.

n, e, f, d	**1**	an..........	**2**	he..........
	3	on.........	**4**	of..........
e, k, b, t	**5**	at..........	**6**	an..........
	7	in.........	**8**	so.........
t, y, p, k	**9**	man......	**10**	sin.........
	11	fee.........	**12**	rum.......
g, e, t, k	**13**	strip......	**14**	ten.........
	15	wee.........	**16**	son........
k, d, h, t	**17**	sea.......	**18**	fin..........
	19	bat.........	**20**	spar.......
h, n, e, d	**21**	kin.........	**22**	mow.......
	23	was.........	**24**	hid..........
k, l, n, m	**25**	zoo.......	**26**	fee.........
	27	law.........	**28**	san.........
l, e, p, n	**29**	tow.......	**30**	bow........
	31	hop.........	**32**	ram.......
h, y, t, n	**33**	car.........	**34**	see.........
	35	pus.........	**36**	rub.........

Now try using each letter at the beginning of the word.

s, b, c, p	**37**	........hare	**38**	........rice
	39	.......less	**40**	.......lamp
s, b, d, p	**41**	........rum	**42**	.......pelt
	43	......lump	**44**	.......lock
b, s, t, g	**45**	........rate	**46**	........kill
	47	......hatch	**48**	.......lend

© Peter Howard 2011   Published by Coroneos Publications

Mixed Double Sounds

Complete each word by using a pair of letters.

Cross out each pair as you use them.

ow ee ea ai oa ei oo ou

1   A mouse has a long, thin t…………l.

2   An Eskimo rides on a sl…………gh.

3   A cr………. is a black bird.

4   A house has many r…………ms.

5   My c……………t keeps me warm in winter.

6   There are seven days in a w…………k.

7   We get h…………t from the sun.

8   Seeds are planted in the gr…………nd.

ie oo aw ur ir ar

9   Dad wears a t…………… around his neck.

10 We can play on the swings in the p…………k.

11 Baby eats her dinner with a sp…………n.

12 My sister has a c……………l in her hair.

13 A dog has four p…………s.

14 The cowboy wore a red sh………t.

Word Sounds

Read each group of three words. Two of the words have the same sound or rhyme.

One word does not rhyme. Write the word that is different on the right.

1	bead	need	bread	....
2	deaf	leaf	reef	....
3	speak	week	break	....
4	meet	great	feet	....
5	cried	field	peeled	....
6	town	flown	mown	....
7	harm	farm	warm	....
8	barn	warn	darn	....
9	plead	tread	speed	....
10	pray	grey	key	....
11	down	gown	shown	....
12	dear	fear	pear	....
13	loud	could	crowd	....
14	steak	sneak	peak	....
15	pour	four	sour	....
16	eight	peek	fete	....
17	ski	stay	free	....

Use the letters on the left to make up the missing words in each sentence.

ea	1	I helped cook a piece of s................. on the barbeque.
ei	2	The bride wore a white v............... in the church.
ey	3	If you mix black and white you get a g.............colour.
ie	4	A t............... broke into the house and stole some money.
ey	5	You will need a k.......... to open the door which is locked.
ye	6	Mum always buys r........... bread at the supermarket.
ew	7	I have learnt to s............ buttons on my clothes.
oe	8	Joe hurt his t............ when he kicked the ball.
oo	9	Mum has a diamond b............. which she wears on her dress.
ol	10	The y......... of a egg is yellow.
ea	11	Your h................. pumps blood to all parts of your body.
oo	12	When it rains hard the river rises and f.............. its banks.
ou	13	Never t................ a power line that has been blown down.
ie	14	My f................. and I are going for a walk together.
al	15	At the zoo I heard a parrot t............ and he said 'Hello Cocky'.
oa	16	Another word for wide is b.................... .
ui	17	One day we are going to move and b............. a new house.

Same Spelling, Different Meaning 1

Can you use the words correctly?

| tip | tip | pot | pot | jet | jet | bit | bit |

1   A .... is a kind of plane.

2   The dog .... the cat on its tail.

3   Dad gave the waiter a .... after our meal.

4   The plant is growing in a ....

5   A .... of water came from the hose.

6   The .... of his nose was red with cold.

7   A .... is part of the reins used in a horse's mouth.

8   In a game of snooker you try to .... the balls.

| cross | cross | bank | date | date | lie |

9   To .... the river you go over the bridge.

10 I will always remember the .... of my birthday.

11 Her horse likes to .... down and roll in mud.

12 My teacher becomes .... if I do not write neatly.

13 I save half my pocket money and put it in a ....

14 The .... is a fruit that grows on a palm tree.

      Published by Coroneos Publications

Write the animal from the box to fit each sentence.

kitten   kid   lamb   fawn   cub   calf

1   A baby sheep is a ....

2   A baby deer is a ....

3   A baby bear is a ....

4   A baby goat is a ....

5   A baby cow is a ....

6   A baby cat is a ....

mare   tiger   cow   pig   ram

7   A .... is kept on a farm to make ham or bacon.

8   We call a female horse over three years old a ....

9   Milk that we drink comes from a ....

10   A father sheep is also called a ....

11   A huge jungle cat with stripes is a ....

deer   camel   hare   zebra   dingo

12   A .... is like a rabbit but its ears are longer.

13   The .... is an African animal like a donkey with stripes.

14   A .... is a wild Australian dog with a sandy colour.

15   The .... is an animal with hoofs. The male has horns or antlers.

16   The .... has long legs and a hump. It lives in the deserts of

Africa and Asia.

Words that Go Together 1

Each word in the box goes with one of the six below. Can you match them?

nest	pail	pan	sticks	string	ball

1	mop	....	2	bat	....
3	kite	....	4	drum	....
5	bird	....	6	stove	....

wax	milk	reel	finger	heat	plant

7	ring	....	8	rod	....
9	bee	....	10	cow	....
11	pot	....	12	sun	....

bang	horns	hoot	wick	sink	shell

13	owl	....	14	tap	....
15	balloon	....	16	bull	....
17	egg	....	18	candle	....

wing	roots	box	wood	barn	head

19	hat	....	20	plant	....
21	axe	....	22	plane	....
23	hay	....	24	lid	....

 Excellence in English Year 2   © Peter Howard 2011   Published by Coroneos Publications

Write a word from the box to fit each sentence.

duster   crayons   paste   chalk   scissors

1 The teacher writes with .... on the blackboard.

2 To clean the blackboard, the teacher uses a ....

3 To colour pictures we use a texta, paints or ....

4 We use .... to stick paper together.

5 .... are useful for cutting out pictures.

Staffroom   playground   staff   pupil   classrooms

6 A child who goes to school is known as a ....

7 The principal and teachers make up the ....

8 A cleaner keeps the .... and corridors clean.

9 Teachers have morning tea and lunch in the ....

10 Boys and girls usually have their lunch in the ....

writing   spell   speak

11 At school we learn how to .... words.

12 We learn to .... better when we discuss things in class.

13 We practise letter shapes to improve our ....

One Word Instead of Several 1

Write one word from the box in place of those in bold print.

> **submarine**   **garage**   **pirate**   **lamely**   **blind**

1   Dad drove his car out of **the place for keeping a car** ....

2   The injured cyclist walked **off with a limp** ....

3   He is from the **ship that can travel under water** ....

4   A person who is **unable to see**, ... walks with a white stick.

5   A **robber on high seas** .... carried a gun or sword.

> **careless**   **melted**   **wardrobe**   **prince**   **droop**

6   Mum keeps her hats in the **place to keep clothes**. ....

7   The **son of the King** .... rode on a white horse.

8   The snow on the ground soon **became water**. ....

9   Her flowers in the vase began to **bend down loosely**. ....

10   Drivers that are **not careful** .... cause accidents.

> **stiff**   **light**   **gaudy**

11   This box of paper clips is **not very heavy**. ....

12   I need some cardboard that is **not easily bent**. ....

13   The dress she wore was **very bright and showy**. ....

Write a word from the box to fit each sentence.

guard   station   driver   ticket   platform

1   To ride on a train we board a carriage at a ....

2   The train stops beside a raised ....

3   All passengers have to buy a .... to travel on a train.

4   The .... makes sure all the doors are closed.

5   The .... sounds a horn in the locomotive before it moves.

lines   goods   mail   bridges   signal

6   When a .... is up or showing a red light, a train must stop.

7   Trains run on railway .... and can change tracks at points.

8   A .... train only carries freight with no passengers.

9   Trains cross over roads at .... or level crossings.

10   Letters and parcels are carried in the .... van.

commuters   berth   dining

11   On long journeys train travellers can eat in the .... car.

12   A bed on a train is called a sleeping ....

13   People who travel to work by train each day are ....

Word Meanings 1

Write a word from the box to match each meaning.

| speck | prong | cell | chill | grip | snack |

1	sharp point	....	2	prison room	....
3	hold tightly	....	4	make cold	....
5	tiny spot	....	6	small meal	....

| fetch | fade | buy | plank | peel | scatter |

7	get by paying	....	8	grow dim	....
9	long flat wood	....	10	spread out	....
11	go and get	....	12	skin of fruit	....

| sure | often | near | camp | knit | plod |

13	make things of wool	....	14	live in a tent	....
15	walk slowly	....	16	many times	....
17	quite certain	....	18	close by	....

| bog | couple | mince | bangle |

19	soft, damp ground	....	20	cut up finely	....
21	a bracelet	....	22	two of a kind	....

    © Peter Howard 2011   Published by Coroneos Publications

Write a word from the box to fit each sentence.

unit   two-storey   cottage   terrace   caravan

1   A .... is a small house.

2   A .... is a home in a high-rise building.

3   A .... house is joined to others in the same street.

4   A .... is a home on wheels.

5   A .... home has rooms upstairs and downstairs.

kitchen   garage   bathroom   laundry

6   A car goes under a carport or in a ....

7   The washing is done in the ....

8   The room used for cooking is the ....

9   A .... is where you can have a shower or bath.

tiles   timber   chimney

10 Most homes are made of brick with .... wall frames.

11 An open fire means the house needs a ....

12 Most roofs of houses are made of iron or ....

Same Spelling, Different Meaning 2

Can you use the words correctly?

kid kid lap lap hit hit duck duck

1   You must .... your head when going through the door.

2   A .... is another word for a child.

3   My cat likes to .... up milk from a saucer.

4   At tennis you .... the ball with a racket.

5   A baby goat is called a ....

6   A song that is a .... is one that sells many copies.

7   The mother was holding a baby on her ....

8   If you do not score any runs at cricket you make a ....

port   port   sack   just   just

9   I have .... finished writing a short story.

10   Mum bought a whole .... of potatoes at the market.

11   The ship came into .... to unload its cargo.

12   Dad was given a bottle of .... for his birthday.

13   The burglar was given a .... sentence for his crime.

Write a word from the box to fit each sentence.

fighter   seaplane   bomber   jumbo   glider

1   A .... jet carries many passengers.

2   A .... is a large plane used by the Air Force in a war.

3   A .... is a small plane made to shoot down other planes.

4   A .... has no engine and must be towed up high.

5   A .... has floats instead of wheels.

officer   radar   captain   flight attendant   gear

6   The .... is the chief pilot who flies a big jet.

7   A .... serves meals and looks after passengers.

8   The first .... also helps fly a big jet.

9   The wheels of a plane are part of the landing............ .

10   The pilot can see in foggy weather with the help of ....

throttle   cockpit   instruments

11   One or two pilots sit in the .... of a plane.

12   A pilot must keep his eyes on the ....

13   To make a plane go faster a pilot moves the ....

Words that Go Together 2

Each word in the box goes with one of the six below.

Can you match them?

horn	grunt	sky	brush	sock	cage

1	moon	....	2	pig	....
3	bird	....	4	paint	....
5	car	....	6	shoe	....

brake	play	belt	foot	pod	drink

7	thong	....	8	cup	....
9	waist	....	10	toy	....
11	car	....	12	pea	....

lion	flowers	book	crust	tree	fish

13	spring	....	14	pie	....
15	roar	....	16	fin	....
17	page	....	18	bark	....

dog	rays	eggs	beach

19	bacon	....	20	sand	....
21	paw	....	22	sun	....

Write a word from the box to fit each sentence.

purrs   tabby   whiskers   tortoiseshell   ginger

1   A .... cat has a striped coat.

2   Most .... cats are males.

3   Most .... cats are females.

4   Cats feel their way at night by using their ....

5   When a cat is happy it ....

bristle   prowl   pounce   stretch   doze

6   Most of the time a cat will .... during the day.

7   At night cats like to .... around.

8   If a cat is hunting it will creep up and .... on a mouse or bird.

9   When a cat wakes up it will .... its limbs .

10 To make itself look fierce a cat will .... its fur.

basket   lick   scratch

11 To wash, a cat will .... its own fur.

12 At home, most cat owners have a .... for their pet.

13 Kittens may .... when you play with them but they do not mean

to hurt you.

One Word Instead of Several 2

Write one word from the box in place of those in bold print.

crockery	actor	foam	crew	beard

1   An old man in the train had **a lot of hair on his face** ....

2   Mum is buying **plates and cups** .... for our caravan.

3   The **persons who work on the ship** .... came ashore.

4   The **man in the film** .... was made up to look like a monster.

5   Waves at the beach make **lots of bubbles** .... on the water.

chased	knelt	crossed	smashed	bled

6   The page **went down on his knees** .... before the king.

7   In the crash one window was **broken to pieces**. ....

8   The chicken **went to the other side of** .... the road.

9   Our dog **ran after** .... the cat that lived next door.

10   After cutting himself, Harry **lost blood** .... from his hand.

hedge	sentry	rascal

11   My baby brother is a **mischievous person**. ....

12   The gardener was cutting the **row of even shrubs** ....

13   A **soldier keeping watch** stood outside the palace door. ....

Write a word from the box to fit each sentence.

nurse   surgeon   matron   doctor   patient

1   A person who is in a hospital is a ....

2   A .... looks after people who are in hospital.

3   The .... is in charge of all the hospital staff.

4   A resident .... finds out what is wrong with you.

5   A .... may come to perform an operation.

syringe   X-ray   thermometer   anaesthetic   stethoscope

6   A .... is used to take your temperature.

7   The doctor listens to your heart and chest with a ....

8   To put you to sleep, a doctor may give you an ....

9   To give you an injection, a nurse will use a ....

10 If you have a broken bone it will show up in an ....

appendix   fractured   mumps

11 If you have .... your neck will be aching and swollen.

12 It is quite common to go to the hospital to have your .... out.

13 If your arm or leg is .... you must go to have it set

in plaster.

Word Meanings 2

Write a word from the box to match each meaning.

soar	thud	oval	now	dusk	stir

1   dull, heavy sound   2   nearly dark ....

3   at present   4   begin to move ....

5   fly high   6   shaped like an egg ....

lantern	wink	express	nap	crunch	twig

7   open and close an eye   8   small branch ....

9   lamp you can carry   10   short sleep ....

11   crush noisily   12   very fast ....

exit	nest	stroll	bunk	chum	rear

13   walk slowly   14   a friend ....

15   a way out   16   a bird's home ....

17   a bed on a ship   18   at the back ....

false	zero	waddle	moose

19   nothing   20   a large deer ....

21   not true   22   walk like a duck ....

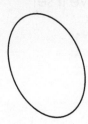

© Peter Howard 2011   Published by Coroneos Publications

6 Using One Vowel

1 web **2** pig **3** cot **4** bat **5** pot **6** mop **7** fox **8** sun **9** van **10** hen **11** pen **12** lid **13** bed **14** rat **15** log **16** fin **17** fat **18** top **19** flag **20** golf **21** nest **22** plum **23** belt **24** skin **25** pram **26** steps **27** swim **28** pond **29** skunk

7 Using One Long Vowel

1 cane **2** tube **3** nine **4** pole **5** bite **6** date **7** mule **8** blade **9** cubes, dice **10** grape, vine **11** bone, rose **12** five, cage **13** plate, cake **14** tune, flute **15** brakes, bike **16** joke, nose

8 Using Two Vowels

1 heel **2** beef **3** tree **4** sheet **5** tea **6** beak **7** cream **8** feast **9** goat **10** soap **11** foal **12** throat **13** shout **14** cloud **15** couch **16** flour **17** train **18** snail **19** rain **20** bait **21** coin **22** boil **23** coil **24** point **25** wool **26** book **27** hood **28** tool **29** Paul **30** launch **31** haul **32** sauce

9 Using One Vowel and Another Letter

1 shark **2** star **3** sharp **4** scarf **5** barber **6** herbs **7** river **8** fern **9** girl **10** thirty **11** skirt **12** dirty **13** crow **14** snow **15** pillow **16** yellow **17** fawn **18** claw **19** lawn **20** hawk **21** owl **22** growl **23** crown **24** towel **25** cork **26** stork **27** north **28** fork **29** tray **30** stay **31** play **32** hay

10 Begin Words by Blending Two Letters Together

1 glass **2** dress **3** spider **4** stump **5** plug **6** cross **7** frowns **8** flippers **9** drives **10** spanner **11** clubs **12** glider **13** stag **14** brush

11 End Words by Blending Two Letters Together

1 duck **2** tank **3** mask **4** chest **5** bang **6** tent **7** dish **8** bitch **9** sock, each **10** Fresh, bush **11** drink, pant **12** watch, first **13** wink, blinking **14** black, ring

12 Make New Words

1 and **2** hen **3** one **4** off **5** ate **6** ant **7** ink **8** sob **9** many **10** sink **11** feet **12** rump **13** stripe **14** tent **15** week **16** song **17** seat **18** find **19** bath **20** spark **21** kind **22** mown **23** wash **24** hide **25** zoom **26** feel **27** lawn **28** sank **29** town **30** bowl **31** hope **32** ramp **33** cart **34** seen **35** push **36** ruby **37** share **38** price **39** bless **40** clamp **41** drum **42** spelt **43** plump **44** block **45** grate **46** skill **47** thatch **48** blend

13 Mixed Double Sounds

1 tail **2** sleigh **3** crow **4** rooms **5** coat **6** week **7** heat **8** ground **9** tie **10** park **11** spoon **12** curl **13** paws **14** shirt

14 Word Sounds

1 bread **2** deaf **3** break **4** great **5** cried **6** town **7** warm **8** warn **9** tread **10** key **11** shown **12** pear **13** could **14** steak **15** sour **16** peek **17** stay

15 Harder Letter Combinations

1 steak **2** veil **3** grey **4** thief **5** key **6** rye **7** sew **8** toe **9** brooch **10** yolk **11** heart **12** floods **13** touch **14** friend **15** talk **16** broad **17** build

16 Same Spelling, Different Meaning 1

1 jet **2** bit **3** tip **4** pot **5** jet **6** tip **7** bit **8** pot **9** cross **10** date **11** lie **12** cross **13** bank **14** date

17 Animals

1 lamb **2** fawn **3** cub **4** kid **5** calf **6** kitten **7** pig **8** mare **9** cow **10** ram **11** tiger **12** hare **13** zebra **14** dingo **15** deer **16** camel

18 Words that Go Together 1

1 pail **2** ball **3** string **4** sticks **5** nest **6** pan **7** finger **8** reel **9** wax **10** milk **11** plant **12** heat **13** hoot **14** sink **15** bang **16** horns **17** shell **18** wick **19** head **20** roots **21** wood **22** wing **23** barn **24** box

Answers

19 School

1 chalk **2** duster **3** crayons **4** paste **5** scissors **6** pupil **7** staff **8** classrooms **9** staffroom **10** playground **11** spell **12** speak **13** writing

20 One Word Instead of Several 1

1 garage **2** lamely **3** submarine **4** blind **5** pirate **6** wardrobe **7** prince **8** melted **9** droop **10** careless **11** light **12** stiff **13** gaudy

21 Train Travel

1 station **2** platform **3** ticket **4** guard **5** driver **6** signal **7** lines **8** goods **9** bridges **10** mail **11** dining **12** berth **13** commuters

22 Word Meanings 1

1 prong **2** cell **3** grip **4** chill **5** speck **6** snack **7** buy **8** fade **9** plank **10** scatter **11** fetch **12** peel **13** knit **14** camp **15** plod **16** often **17** sure **18** near **19** bog **20** mince **21** bangle **22** couple

23 Homes

1 cottage **2** unit **3** terrace **4** caravan **5** two-storey **6** garage **7** laundry **8** kitchen **9** bathroom **10** timber **11** chimney **12** tiles

24 Same Spelling, Different Meaning 2

1 duck **2** kid **3** lap **4** hit **5** kid **6** hit **7** lap **8** duck **9** just **10** sack **11** port **12** port **13** just

25 Aeroplanes

1 jumbo **2** bomber **3** fighter **4** glider **5** seaplane **6** captain **7** flight attendant **8** officer **9** gear **10** radar **11** cockpit **12** instruments **13** throttle

26 Words that Go Together 2

1 sky **2** grunt **3** cage **4** brush **5** horn **6** sock **7** foot **8** drink **9** belt **10** play **11** brake **12** pod **13** flowers **14** crust **15** lion **16** fish **17** book **18** tree **19** eggs **20** beach **21** dog **22** rays

27 Cats

1 tabby **2** ginger **3** tortoiseshell **4** whiskers **5** purrs **6** doze **7** prowl **8** pounce **9** stretch **10** bristle **11** lick **12** basket **13** scratch

28 One Word Instead of Several 2

1 beard **2** crockery **3** crew **4** actor **5** foam **6** knelt **7** smashed **8** crossed **9** chased **10** bled **11** rascal **12** hedge **13** sentry

29 In Hospital

1 patient **2** nurse **3** matron **4** doctor **5** surgeon **6** thermometer **7** stethoscope **8** anaesthetic **9** syringe **10** x-ray **11** mumps **12** appendix **13** fractured

30 Word Meanings 2

1 thud **2** dusk **3** now **4** stir **5** soar **6** oval **7** wink **8** twig **9** lantern **10** nap **11** crunch **12** express **13** stroll **14** chum **15** exit **16** nest **17** bunk **18** rear **19** zero **20** moose **21** false **22** waddle

31 At the Zoo

1 keeper **2** ticket **3** entrance **4** kiosk **5** exit **6** leopards **7** apes **8** elephants **9** otters **10** possums **11** poisonous **12** cuddly **13** dangerous

© Peter Howard 2011   Published by Coroneos Publications

32 Same Spelling, Different Meaning 3

1 let **2** wave **3** play **4** run **5** play **6** wave **7** let **8** run **9** swallow **10** prune **11** bar **12** bow **13** prune **14** bow

33 Fires

1 fighter **2** brigade **3** station **4** ladders **5** axe **6** bushfire **7** smoulder **8** smoke **9** crawl **10** radiator **11** tank **12** extinguisher **13** camping

34 Words that Go Together 3

1 broom **2** arm **3** face **4** lace **5** lock **6** light **7** socks **8** pans **9** spider **10** glass **11** silver **12** bottle **13** girl **14** beak **15** stump **16** chair **17** cart **18** suds **19** sheep **20** brush **21** clock **22** trout

35 Riding Horses

1 saddle **2** reins **3** stirrups **4** mount **5** gallops **6** oats **7** pony **8** trots **9** groom **10** stockhorse **11** Shetland **12** gymkhana **13** canters

36 One Word Instead of Several 3

1 price **2** crisp **3** nozzle **4** artist **5** raw **6** glare **7** rouse **8** darn **9** sever **10** drawl **11** rubbish **12** paling **13** shore

37 Fishing

1 reel **2** bait **3** knife **4** sea **5** beach **6** slimy **7** spikes **8** small **9** gaff **10** scales **11** shallow **12** deeper **13** rocky

38 Arranging Words in Groups 1

1 beanies **2** caps **3** helmets **4** coats **5** jackets **6** sweaters **7** gumboots **8** sandals **9** thongs **10** fig **11** orange **12** peach **13** bean **14** carrot **15** pea **16** beef **17** pork **18** veal **19** bark **20** bleat **21** neigh **22** cluck **23** quack **24** tweet **25** cheer **26** moan **27** yell

39 Gardening

1 spade **2** soil **3** fertiliser **4** rake **5** wheelbarrow **6** vegetable **7** fragrant **8** weeds **9** evergreen **10** water **11** bulbs **12** cutting **13** potting

40 Word Meanings 3

1 eel **2** harvest **3** seldom **4** poultry **5** ignorant **6** tart **7** crawl **8** gallant **9** grubby **10** trawler **11** ice **12** select **13** carton **14** placid **15** sapling **16** soot **17** rickety **18** voyage **19** prank **20** settee **21** nudge **22** prowl **23** echo **24** explode

41 Arranging Words in Groups 2

1 cry **2** fret **3** weep **4** giggle **5** laugh **6** smile **7** frown **8** rage **9** scowl **10** flaps **11** tail **12** wing **13** deck **14** keel **15** mast **16** bonnet **17** boot **18** gearbox **19** fawn **20** rust **21** tan **22** gold **23** lemon **24** straw **25** lily **26** milk **27** snow

42 Shopping

1 pair **2** florist **3** leg **4** jar **5** packet **6** café **7** loaf **8** chemist **9** hardware **10** box **11** antique **12** sports **13** jeweller's

43 Same Spelling, Different Meaning 4

1 down **2** beat **3** roll **4** beat **5** down **6** roll **7** mean **8** mean **9** game **10** pick **11** log **12** block **13** log **14** game **15** pick

44 At the Circus

1 tent **2** tricks **3** tamer **4** flames **5** trapeze **6** balance **7** band **8** ringmaster **9** walkers **10** funny **11** spotlight **12** bareback **13** artists

45 Words that Go Together 4

1 lamb **2** Indian **3** wire **4** miner **5** beetle **6** bone **7** sleeping **8** dune **9** shark **10** glue **11** brood **12** church **13** cream **14** snare **15** wharf **16** hoist **17** swan **18** wealth **19** caught **20** heart **21** vine **22** brooch **23** plough **24** dough

Answers

46 One Word Instead of Several 4
1 moist 2 mimic 3 hollow 4 deliver 5 strict 6 splutter 7 numb 8 grumble 9 wary 10 ripple 11 panic 12 gravel

47 Word Meanings 4
1 beacon 2 ferry 3 warble 4 lurch 5 detest 6 drizzle 7 totter 8 eager 9 tablet 10 increase 11 hatchet 12 ignore 13 adore 14 erect 15 bleak 16 linger 17 inhale 18 cluster 19 sturdy 20 bedraggled 21 punctual 22 descend 23 bleached 24 flexible

48 Dogs
1 mongrel 2 Dalmatian 3 Dachshund 4 heeler 5 spaniel 6 vet 7 kennel 8 watch 9 snarl 10 muzzle 11 slobbers 12 scent 13 obey

49 Arranging Words in Groups 3
1 evil 2 naughty 3 wicked 4 giant 5 huge 6 vast 7 fine 8 great 9 pure 10 afraid 11 scared 12 timid 13 brief 14 little 15 tiny 16 fine 17 handsome 18 lovely 19 foolish 20 stupid 21 unwise 22 brainy 23 skilful 24 smart 25 aged 26 ancient 27 elderly

50 Books
1 title 2 chapters 3 cover 4 author 5 poet 6 goblin 7 hero 8 heroine 9 courtier 10 wizard 11 dictionary 12 atlas 13 text

51 Where Are the Notices?
1 on someone's front gate 2 at the beach 3 at a petrol station 4 at a railway station 5 at the zoo 6 in the library 7 on a bridge crossing a river 8 on a farm gate 9 in a shopping centre 10 on a blank wall 11 in a shop window

52 The Golden Egg
1 market 2 golden 3 cut 4 two 5 yes

53 Which Word is Different?
1 buns 2 oil 3 sandals 4 snail 5 ride 6 picture 7 cow 8 glove 9 cabbage 10 bright 11 fork 12 tiny 13 frail 14 dull 15 iceberg 16 canary 17 classroom

54 The Ants and the Grasshopper
1 summer 2 rooms 3 cold 4 eat 5 no 6 yes

55 Little Words
1 at 2 by 3 of 4 on 5 for 6 their 7 to 8 off 9 with 10 too 11 I 12 there 13 on 14 me 15 two

56 The Three Fishes
first saw fish net had he top catch fisherman

57 Similar Sentences
1 Steven was feeling very sick. 2 The bread was extremely hard. 3 The burglar stood quite still. 4 You will be hearing from me tomorrow. 5 His face went a bright red colour. 6 At seven o'clock the train arrives.

58 Opposite Sentences
1 Charles was idle all day. 2 Mary felt very hungry at the time. 3 His house was large but dirty. 4 All the guests were glad to leave the party. 5 She seemed to be in form that day. 6 Mr Basham showed nothing but kindness.

59 Eating Fruit
1 sugar 2 yes 3 yes 4 apple 5 banana 6 11 7 dates

60 Days and Months of the Year
1 Tuesday 2 Wednesday 3 December 4 August 5 4 6 7 7 Wednesday 8 June 9 Tuesday

Write a word from the box to fit each sentence.

entrance exit ticket keeper kiosk

1   A person who looks after animals is a ....

2   Before entering the zoo you must buy a ....

3   The gate you first go through to enter is called the ....

4   If you want to buy anything to eat or drink you go to a ....

5   The gate from which you leave the zoo is the ....

otters possums leopards elephants apes

6   Lions, tigers, jaguars, cheetahs and .... are all large cats.

7   Gorillas, chimpanzees and orang-outangs are all ....

8   The largest of the animals in the zoo are the ....

9   Besides seals, you will probably see .... swimming.

10   The .... are native tree-climbers from Australia.

cuddly dangerous poisonous

11   Many snakes are .... so they are kept behind glass.

12   Koalas look like .... teddy bears.

13   The rhinoceros is very .... so his cage

must be strong.

Same Spelling, Different Meaning 3

Can you use the words correctly?

let	let	run	run	play	play	wave	wave

1   I hope my mother will .... me go for a swim today.

2   Each of us can .... a little flag when the Queen arrives.

3   To .... cricket you must have a bat.

4   A winger must .... fast with the ball in a rugby match.

5   In the school .... I was one of the three wise men.

6   A .... broke against our boat and made us all wet.

7   The house has been to .... since it was sold.

8   There is enough room in the backyard for a chicken ....

bow	bow	bar	swallow	prune	prune

9   The baby must be careful not to .... that button.

10 Mother will .... the roses in the middle of winter.

11 Some concrete blocks have been placed there to .... traffic.

12 Sally wears a .... in her hair.

13 A .... is a dried plum.

14 Robin Hood used to shoot with a .... and arrow.

Write a word from the box to fit each sentence.

station   axe   brigade   fighter   ladders

1   A fire .... helps put out fires with hoses.

2   He or she is a member of the fire ....

3   The fire engine is kept at the fire ....

4   To reach tall buildings, fire fighters use long ....

5   They smash doors or windows with an .... to rescue people.

smoulder   bushfire   radiator   smoke   crawl

6   A .... burns grass and trees in the country.

7   Fires that burn without flames just ....

8   Breathing .... in a house on fire can kill you.

9   To avoid smoke, you should .... along the floor.

10   Be careful that your clothes do not touch a heater or ....

extinguisher   camping   tank

11   Fire fighters can walk through smoke if they have an oxygen ....

12   Every house should have a small fire ....

13   When .... , make sure the fire is put out each day.

Words that Go Together 3

Each word in the box goes with one of the six below.

Can you match them?

lock	broom	arm	lace	light	face

1	witch	....	2	hand	....
3	nose	....	4	shoe	....
5	key	....	6	lamp	....

bottle	silver	pans	glass	spider	socks

7	shoes	....	8	pots	....
9	web	....	10	window	....
11	gold	....	12	cork	....

chair	stump	girl	suds	cart	beak

13	dress	....	14	bird	....
15	cricket	....	16	table	....
17	horse	....	18	soap	....

trout	clock	brush	sheep

19	wool	....	20	hair	....
21	time	....	22	stream	....

Write a word from the box to fit each sentence.

gallops   reins   stirrups   saddle   mount

1   You sit on a .... when you ride a horse.

2   To guide a horse you use .... which you hold.

3   Your feet fit into the .... which hang from straps.

4   You .... a horse when you get on its back.

5   When a horse .... it is running fast.

pony   oats   stockhorse   groom   trots

6   When a horse is not grazing it must be fed .... or hay.

7   A small horse suitable for children to ride is a ....

8   A horse .... when it is going a little faster than a walk.

9   To .... a horse is to brush and clean it.

10   The .... is used for rounding up cattle.

gymkhana   Shetland   canters

11   One breed of very small pony is a ....

12   A horse-riding competition is called a ....

13   A horse .... when it goes a little faster than a trot.

One Word Instead of Several 3

Write one word from the box in place of those in italics.

nozzle   artist   price   crisp   raw

1 The *amount of money paid* .... for lunch was $4.

2 The sliced potatoes were *firm but easily broken.* ....

3 Water rushed from the *spout of the hose.* ....

4 Henry is an Aboriginal *person who draws or paints.* ....

5 Meat that was *not cooked* was fed to the crocodile. ....

darn   rouse   glare   drawl   sever

6 *To look angrily at someone* is to ....

7 *To wake someone up* is to .... them.

8 *To repair a hole in something* is to .... it.

9 *To cut something off* is to .... it.

10 *To speak in a slow and lazy way* is to ....

shore   rubbish   paling

11 He threw the *waste material* .... into the bin.

12 A .... fence is *made from strips of wood.*

13 Her house is on the *land next to the lake.* ....

Write a word from the box to fit each sentence.

sea   beach   reel   knife   bait

1   Most people fish with a rod and ....

2   They need a hook, sinker and ....

3   A .... is handy to cut the line or clean fish.

4   Some people have boats so they can go deep ....fishing.

5   Others are happy to fish from rocks or the ....

spikes   small   gaff   scales   slimy

6   The skin of all fish is .... when they are caught.

7   Be careful, as some fish have sharp teeth or ....

8   You must throw fish back that are very ....

9   A strong hook with a long handle to pull fish into a boat is a ....

10   Before cooking a fish you must scrape the .... off its skin.

shallow   rocky   deeper

11   You can catch whiting over .... sand banks.

12   Flathead live in .... water over a sandy bottom.

13   Snapper are caught in water where there is a .... bottom.

Arranging Words in Groups 1

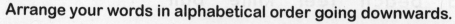

There are nine words in each box. Three belong in each group.

Write the words in columns under the headings.

Arrange your words in alphabetical order going downwards.

caps   sweaters   thongs   jackets   helmets
coats   gumboots   beanies   sandals

hats		clothes		footwear
1	4	....	7	....
2	5	....	8	....
3	6	....	9	....

peach   pork   bean   orange   veal   fig
beef   pea   carrot

fruit		vegetables		meat
10	14	....	17	....
11	15	....	18	....
12	16	....	19	....

bleat   cheer   cluck   neigh   quack
bark   yell   moan   tweet

sounds made by animals		sounds made by birds		sounds made by people
19	22	....	25	....
20	23	....	26	....
21	24	....	27	....

Write a word from the box to fit each sentence.

soil   wheelbarrow   rake   fertilizer   spade

1   To plant flowers or shrubs you dig with a ....

2   All plants need good .... to grow.

3   They also need to be given plant food or ....

4   A .... is used in the garden to gather up leaves and sticks.

5   Every gardener needs a .... to carry things.

evergreen   water   vegetable   weeds   fragrant

6   You will see lettuce and onions growing in a .... garden.

7   Roses are .... flowers that are easy to grow.

8   To keep garden beds tidy you must pull out the ....

9   Some trees that do not lose their leaves are ....

10   When the weather is dry you must .... the garden.

bulbs   potting   cutting

11   Daffodils grow from .... and flower in the spring.

12   To grow a daisy all you need to do is plant a small ....

13   Plants in pots grow best if you use a .... mix.

Word Meanings 3

Write a word from the box to match each meaning.

seldom	poultry	ignorant	tart	eel	harvest

1	fish like a snake	....	2	gather a crop	....
3	not often	....	4	birds we eat	....
5	knowing little	....	6	pastry filled with jam	....

ice	select	gallant	grubby	trawler	crawl

7	move on hands and knees	....	8	brave	....
9	dirty	....	10	fishing boat	....
11	frozen water	....	12	choose	....

soot	carton	placid	rickety	voyage	sapling

13	a box	....	14	calm and peaceful	....
15	a young tree	....	16	black part of smoke	....
17	weak and shaky	....	18	a trip by boat	....

echo	prank	nudge	settee	prowl	explode

19	a trick or a joke	....	20	a long seat	....
21	push with elbow	....	22	look for prey	....
23	sound that is repeated	....	24	blow up	....

There are nine words in each box. Three belong in each group.

Write the words in columns under the headings.

Arrange your words in alphabetical order going downwards.

cry   giggle   frown   rage   laugh
fret   weep   scowl   smile

	sad words		happy words		angry words
1	....	4	....	7	....
2	....	5	....	8	....
3	....	6	....	9	....

boot   deck   flaps   wing   tail
gearbox   keel   bonnet   mast

	part of a plane		part of a ship		part of a car
10	....	13	....	16	....
11	....	14	....	17	....
12	....	15	....	18	....

rust   lemon   milk   lily   straw
snow   tan   gold   fawn

	brown colours		yellow colours		white colours
19	....	22	....	25	....
20	....	23	....	26	....
21	....	24	....	27	....

Shopping

Write a word from the box to fit each sentence.

leg	florist	pair	jar	packet

1   'I think we will buy you a .... of new shoes,' said Mum.

2   'Please may I have a bunch of tulips,' said Jill to the ....

3   'I want a large .... of lamb,' said my uncle to the butcher.

4   In the supermarket we bought a .... of my favourite jam.

5   At the newsagent dad bought a .... of envelopes

box	café	hardware	chemist	loaf

6   After shopping we all had tea and cakes in a ....

7   At the baker's shop Mum bought a large .... of bread.

8   We bought some cough mixture for my sister at the ....

9   My brother bought some glue at the .... store.

10   We needed a .... of matches to light our barbeque.

jeweller's	sports	antique

11   We went into an .... shop to buy an old vase.

12   In the window of the .... store I saw a new tennis racket.

13   My sister liked some earrings in the .... shop.

Same Spelling, Different Meaning 4

Can you use the words correctly?

roll roll beat beat down down mean mean

1 Will you walk .... the path with me to the beach?

2 I hope we .... your team next time we play.

3 Just .... the ball along the ground in a straight line.

4 To make the cake you will have to .... two eggs with butter.

5 The soft feathers of a young bird are called ....

6 The teacher calls the .... before we start working.

7 With no rain, does this .... there will be no wheat this year?

8 A person who is .... does not like spending money.

log log block game game pick pick

9 Tennis is a .... played by two or four persons.

10 I like to .... roses in our garden to put in a vase.

11 Mum asked me to put a .... on the open fire.

12 The newsagent and the post office are in the same ....

13 Every pilot who flies uses a .... book to write about his trip.

14 What a pity hunters still travel to Africa to shoot wild ....!

15 In some countries people still work on roads with

a .... and shovel.

At the Circus

Write a word from the box to fit each sentence.

tricks tamer tent trapeze flames

1   The circus is performed in a huge ....

2   Acrobats tumble and do ....

3   The lion .... makes the poor cats jump through hoops.

4   A fire-eater blows .... from his mouth.

5   The women who swings on the .... are very skilful.

ringmaster funny band balance walkers

6   A seal is an animal that can .... a ball on its nose.

7   The .... plays loud music with lots of drum beats.

8   The .... wears a black top hat and carries a whip.

9   Tightrope .... carry long sticks to help them.

10 Clowns are ...., as they make us laugh.

artists bareback spotlight

11 As performers come on a .... beams on them.

12 Ladies in pretty costumes ride horses ....

13 A net is used in case the .... fall from up high.

Each word in the box goes with one of the six below.

Can you match them?

lamb   Indian   wire   bone   miner   beetle

1	bleat	....	2	chief	....	
3	fence	....	4	coal	....	
5	drone	....	6	spine	....	

dune   brood   glue   shark   church   sleeping

7	snore	....	8	sand	....	
9	attack	....	10	sticky	....	
11	chickens	....	12	Sunday	....	

wharf   hoist   snare   wealth   swan   cream

13	cake	....	14	rabbit	....	
15	ships	....	16	washing	....	
17	lake	....	18	yacht	....	

vine   brooch   dough   heart   caught   plough

19	catcher	....	20	blood	....	
21	grape	....	22	diamond	....	
23	tractor	....	24	bread	....	

One Word Instead of Several 4

Write one word from the box in place of those in bold print.

| hollow | strict | mimic | moist | deliver |

1   The swimming costume was **slightly wet**. ....

2   To **copy someone for fun** is to .... them.

3   The old log was **empty inside**. ....

4   Please **hand over** .... this message I have written.

5   One teacher at our school is **stern and severe**. ....

| ripple | numb | wary | splutter | grumble |

6   Bob was so surprised that all he could do was make **spitting sounds** ....

7   My feet were **without any feeling** .... as it was so cold.

8   The old man does nothing but **mutter and complain** ....

9   You should be **on the lookout for danger** .... if a stranger talks to you.

10 There was not even a **tiny wave** .... on the ocean.

| gravel | panic |

11 **Sudden terror and alarm** .... broke out at the news.

12 The driveway was made of **small pebbles and sand**. ....

Write a word from the box to match each meaning.

warble   beacon   drizzle   lurch   ferry   detest

1	signal light	....	2	type of boat	....
3	sing like a bird	....	4	roll to one side	....
5	hate very much	....	6	rain in small drops	....

totter   ignore   hatchet   tablet   increase   eager

7	walk with shaky steps	....	8	very keen	....
9	a pill	....	10	make greater	....
11	small axe	....	12	take no notice	....

linger   inhale   adore   cluster   bleak   erect

13	love very much	....	14	straight up	....
15	cold and dismal	....	16	stay on	....
17	draw into the lungs	....	18	be in a bunch	....

descend   flexible   bleached   bedraggled   punctual   sturdy

19	strong	....	20	wet and dirty	....
21	on time	....	22	go down	....
23	made white	....	24	easily bent	....

Dogs

Write a word from the box to fit each sentence.

spaniel   Dachshund   mongrel   Dalmatian   heeler

1   A .... dog is a mixture of breeds.

2   The .... is spotted black and white.

3   A .... is often called a sausage dog.

4   Farmers in Australia often have a kelpie or a blue ....

5   The .... is a dog with a curly coat and floppy ears.

kennel   muzzle   vet   snarl   watch

6   You take a dog that is sick or injured to a ....

7   A special small house made for a dog is a ....

8   A .... dog is kept to keep away burglars.

9   An angry dog may .... and bite.

10 To keep a dog from biting people you put a .... on it.

obey   scent   slobbers

11 When a dog pants and is thirsty it ....

12 A dog follows the .... of something it tries to find.

13 A well-trained dog will .... you when you speak to it.

There are nine words in each box. Three belong in each group.

Write the words in columns under the headings.

Arrange your words in alphabetical order going downwards.

great   huge   naughty   vast   fine
wicked   pure   evil   giant

words for bad	words for big	words for good
1	4	7 ....
2	5	8 ....
3	6	9 ....

tiny   lovely   timid   brief   scared
fine   handsome   little   afraid

words for frightened	words for small	words for nice
10	14	17 ....
11	15	18 ....
12	16	19 ....

stupid   aged   smart   brainy   foolish
unwise   elderly   ancient   skilful

words for silly	words for clever	words for old
19	22	25 ....
20	23	26 ....
21	24	27 ....

Books

Write a word from the box to fit each sentence.

chapters	cover	author	title	poet

1   The name of a book is called the ....

2   A book is divided up into a number of ....

3   The outside of a book is the ....

4   The person who writes a book is the ....

5   A person who writes verses that rhyme is a ....

courtier	wizard	hero	heroine	goblin

6   Fairy tales often have a giant, dwarf or a .... in them.

7   The main male person who is not evil in a book is the ....

8   The main female person who is not evil in a book is the ....

9   A person who lives in a palace with a king or queen is a ....

10   There is always a witch or .... in stories about magic.

atlas	dictionary	text

11   You can look up how to spell words in a ....

12   A book full of maps is an ....

13   A .... book teaches you about a subject.

Alongside each notice write where you would most likely see it.

Choose each answer from the ones given below.

1   BEWARE OF THE DOG ....

2   SWIM BETWEEN THE FLAGS ....

3   NO SMOKING BY BOWSERS ....

4   CROSS THE LINES BY THE BRIDGE ....

5   DO NOT FEED THE ANIMALS ....

6   RETURN BOOKS TO THE DESK ....

7   NO FISHING ....

8   BEWARE OF THE BULL ....

9   NO ROLLER SKATING ....

10 POST NO BILLS ....

11 WE ARE CLOSED ....

in the library
on a farm gate
on someone's front gate
in a shopping centre
in a shop window
at the beach
at a petrol station
on a bridge crossing a river
on a blank wall
at a railway station
at the zoo

The Golden Egg

Once upon a time, a man and his wife went to the market. They bought a fat goose. How surprised they were when the goose began to lay an egg made of gold every day!

A week later, the man was talking to his wife. 'Just think of all that gold inside the goose. I think I'll cut the goose open and take all the gold at once.'

When the man cut the bird open, he found it was just like any other goose. "Oh dear,' cried the wife, 'the goose will not lay any more golden eggs for us.' Yes, the man had foolishly killed the goose that laid the golden eggs. I think you will agree that he was too greedy. He should have been quite happy to have one golden egg each day.

Write each missing word. You must use a word from the story.

1   The goose was bought at the ....

2   It laid a .... egg each day.

3   The man .... the bird open.

Answer the question. Use a word or write 'yes' or 'no'.

4   How many people are there in there in the story? ....

5   Does the story tell us not to be hungry or greedy? ....

© Peter Howard 2011   Published by Coroneos Publications

Which Word is Different?

In each row of words one word is not like the other four.

Circle this odd word and write it in the space.

1	lettuce	beans	carrots	buns	potatoes	....
2	lemonade	tea	oil	coffee	milk	....
3	pants	shirt	skirt	sandals	blouse	....
4	magpie	snail	crow	sparrow	kookaburra	....
5	race	walk	crawl	run	ride	....
6	sofa	desk	picture	chair	table	....
7	cow	cub	kitten	puppy	lamb	....
8	glove	hand	foot	arm	leg	....
9	apple	peach	cabbage	mango	plum	....
10	yellow	green	bright	blue	purple	....
11	fork	plate	saucer	cup	jug	....
12	big	wide	tiny	huge	great	....
13	solid	sound	firm	frail	tough	....
14	shiny	dull	glowing	glossy	sparkling	....
15	iceberg	planet	meteor	star	comet	....
16	chicken	turkey	duck	hen	canary	....
17	bathroom	laundry	kitchen	classroom	bedroom	....

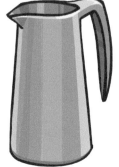

The Ants and the Grasshopper

A nest of ants had been very busy all through the summer. The ants spent their time collecting food. They put the food into little rooms in the nest under ground. When winter came and some snow fell, the ants had plenty to eat.

One very cold day a grasshopper, who was very hungry, came to the ant-hill. He spoke to some of the ants who were keeping watch. He begged them to give him something to eat.

One ant asked the grasshopper how he had spent the summer. The ant also asked if he had saved up any food for the winter.

The grasshopper replied, 'What a pity! I spent all my time singing, playing and dancing. I never thought about winter.'

The ant answered: 'Then we have nothing to give you. People who play all summer must expect to go hungry all winter.'

Write each missing word. You must use a word from the story.

1   The ants collected food during the .... time.

2   The food was put into .... in the nest.

3   The day was .... when the grasshopper met the ants.

4   He asked them for something to ....

Use 'yes' or 'no' to answer the questions.

5   Did the ants help the grasshopper? ....

6   Did the grasshopper spend some time singing? ....

© Peter Howard 2011   Published by Coroneos Publications

Use a little word once in each sentence.

for   of   by   their   on   at   off   to

1   Please meet me ……………………….. the beach tomorrow morning.

2   She lives in a house ………………………. the lake.

3   I had a cup ………………………. tea for breakfast.

4   The cow trod ………………………. the seeds in the garden.

5   A mother dog cares ………………………. her pups.

6   I met the two girls and ……………………….. aunt.

7   We are going ………………………. town in the morning.

8   The lid blew ………………………. the bin in the wind.

too   on   with   I   two   there   me

9   Jim was happy ……………………. his new cricket bat.

10   Sue has a doll and Phillipa has one ……………………….. .

11   Kim and ……………………. are going to the pictures.

12   Donald's new kitten is over ……………………….. .

13   We shall rely ………………………. you to bring the cakes.

14   He gave Tom and ……………………. some old stamps.

15   She had ………………………. dogs at home.

The Three Fishes

Excellence in English Year 2

Write each missing word.

Three fishes lived in a pond. The .... was wise, the second had a little sense, and the third was foolish. A fisherman .... the fish and went for his net.

'I must get out of this pond at once,' said the wise ....

And he threw himself into a little channel that led to a river.

Soon the fisherman came back with his .... He stopped up the channel that led to the river. The second fish wished he .... followed the wise fish. But .... thought of a plan to escape. He floated upside down on .... of the water. The fisherman thought the fish was dead, so he did not bother to .... it. But the foolish fish was caught. The .... took it home to eat. This story tells us that we should all try to be wise.

© Peter Howard 2011   Published by Coroneos Publications

Similar Sentences

Read each group of three sentences.

Write the sentence that is similar to the first one.

1   Steven felt as sick as a dog.

     Steven looked like a sick dog.

     Steven was feeling very sick.

     ....

2   The bread felt as hard as iron.

     The bread was not at all soft.

     The bread was extremely hard.

     ....

3   The burglar froze on the spot.

     The burglar stood quite still.

     The burglar moves on to the frozen pond.

     ....

4   I shall telephone you tomorrow.

     I shall be using the telephone tomorrow.

     You will be hearing from me tomorrow.

     ....

5   His face went as red as a cherry.

     His face was the shape of a cherry.

     His face went a bright red colour.

     ....

6   The train is due at seven o'clock.

     At seven o'clock the train arrives.

     The train departs at seven o'clock.

     ....

Opposite Sentences

Read each group of three sentences.

One sentence is the opposite of the other two.

Write the opposite sentence below.

1   Charles was very busy all day.

Charles had no time to himself all day.

Charles was idle for the whole day.

....

2   Mary had no appetite for the food.

Mary did not feel like eating at all.

Mary felt very hungry at the time.

....

3   His house was small but clean.

His house was tiny but neat.

His house was large but dirty.

....

4   At the party everyone had a great time.

All the guests were glad to leave the party.

The visitors very much enjoyed the party.

....

5   She had an off day during her match.

She seemed to be in form that day.

She did not play as well as usual.

....

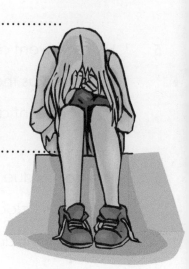

6   Mr Basham was known for his cruelty.

Mr Basham was extremely brutal.

Me Basham showed nothing but kindness.

....

Fruit is a food that is very good for us to eat. From fruit our bodies get sugar that we need. This sugar is better for us than the sugar we can buy in packets. The sugar in lollies is also not as good for us.

Lemons, oranges and grapefruit give us lots of vitamins we need. Prunes and dates gives us iron. Our bodies need these things to help us grow strong and healthy.

Do you like eating apples? If you do, then your body will be getting a good food. An apple also helps clean your teeth if your toothbrush is not handy. Try to finish your lunch at school by eating an apple. This will help to stop your teeth from getting holes in them.

Other fruits that are good for you are pineapples, pears, peaches, apricots and bananas.

Answer each question with one word or use 'yes' or 'no'.

1   What do you think lollies are mainly made of? ....

2   Are there vitamins that we need in an orange? ....

3   Do our bodies need vitamins to grow? ....

4   What kind of a fruit helps clean your teeth? ....

5   Write a long yellow fruit that is mentioned. ....

6   How many kinds of fruit are mentioned in the story? ....

7   From which fruit that grows on a palm tree do we get iron? ....

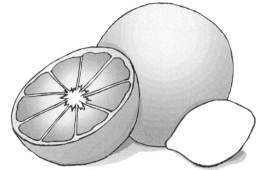

Days and Months of the Year

Days of the Week
Sunday
Monday
Tuesday
Wednesday
Thursday
Friday
Saturday

Months of the Year	
January	July
February	August
March	September
April	October
May	November
June	December

Thirty days has September, April, June and November. All the rest have thirty-one except February alone, which has twenty-eight days clear, with one more each leap year.

1 What day comes between Monday and Wednesday? ....

2 Which day comes in the middle of a school week? ....

3 What is the last month of the year? ....

4 What is the eighth month of the year? ....

5 How many months have thirty days? ....

6 How many months have thirty-one days? ....

7 If June 29th was a Saturday, on what day of the week would July 3rd fall?

   ....

8 What is the shortest month in the year beginning with the letter J?

   ....

9 If December 14th is a Friday, on what day of the week

   will Christmas Day fall? ....

   © Peter Howard 2011   Published by Coroneos Publications